I0480841

The virtual meeting guidebook

If you can control the media, success is up to the skills you already have

Dr. Macedonio Alanis

Imprint

Any Brand names and product names mentioned in this book are subject to trademark, Brand or patent protection, and trademarks or registered trademarks of their respective holders. The use of brand names, product names, common names, trade names, product descriptions, etc. even without a particular marking in this work is in no way to be construed to mean that such names may be regarded as unrestricted in respect of trademark and brand protection legislation and could thus be used by anyone.

Cover image photo by Vadim Sherbakov on Unsplash

ISBN-13: 9798688486971

https://www.amazon.com/-/e/B08529L1PZ

Copyright © 2020 Macedonio Alanis

Dedication

For the road warrior inside all of us, may business in the new world be more prosperous than ever before

Table of Contents

Extended Table of Contents

Chapter 1

Why do We Need Virtual Meetings?

"It was the best of times, it was the worst of times, it was the age of wisdom, it was the age of foolishness, it was the epoch of belief, it was the epoch of incredulity, it was the season of Light, it was the season of Darkness, it was the spring of hope, it was the winter of despair, we had everything before us, we had nothing before us, we were all going direct to Heaven, we were all going direct the other way—in short, the period was so far like the present period, that some of its noisiest authorities insisted on its being received, for good or for evil, in the superlative degree of comparison only."

Charles Dickens, "A Tale of Two Cities," 1859

1.1- There are winners and losers in any revolution

You are the best in the business. No one leaves your meetings without buying into your ideas. You close million-dollar deals for breakfast and can tell a person's intentions just by the strength of their handshake. Suddenly, the rules of business change. Now you have to present your ideas sitting at a computer at home. The technology is called videoconferencing, and while the final objective remains the same (to make money), your skills feel outdated. Welcome to the twenty-first century.

A videoconference lets you talk to customers or coworkers in different locations. It saves time and travel expenses and gives you almost infinite reach. The price for those benefits is a change in some of the basic rules of business that you used to know and follow.

There is no more handshake, you will not be able to smell fear in your counterparts, and signatures will eventually become a series of unreadable symbols.

Yet, as foreign as a videoconference might seem, your goals are the same. The negotiating tactics and selling methods have not changed. Only the media is different.

Whether today's business environment becomes "the spring of hope" or "the winter of despair" depends on how prepared you are. Remote meetings have been part of business since the days of telephone conferences. People have developed techniques to leverage their strengths and overcome their difficulties.

Success depends on more than just knowing how to talk, negotiate, or sell. It is also essential to understand and control technology. It would be best if you became an expert at organizing remote meetings, managing people in their own homes, and looking good on a small screen.

The objective of this book is to present tips, tools, and techniques to help you plan, organize, and manage remote meetings. If you can control the media, then it will be up to the negotiating, management, or selling skills that you already have to lead you to success.

1.2- What is a videoconference?

The idea of holding a meeting with people in different locations has different names: videoconference, web conference, or virtual meeting.

The Merriam-Webster Dictionary defines a videoconference as "the holding of a conference among people at remote locations by means of transmitted audio and video signals" [Merriam-Webster, 2020].

The Cambridge Dictionary defines "a system with video cameras connected by the internet or by a special connection so that people in different places can see and communicate with each other, so they do not have to travel to meetings" [Cambridge Dictionary, 2020].

Wikipedia defines "Web conferencing" as "an umbrella term for various types of online conferencing and collaborative services, including webinars ("web seminars"), webcasts, and web meetings." [Wikipedia, 2020] The site specifies that the reunions can be one-to-one, one-to-many, or many-to-many.

Some academic papers use the term "virtual meetings" to refer to working encounters among people in different locations. The reports analyze the requirements for successful virtual meetings and the effects of distance on productivity and perception [Rubinger et al., 2020; Fadlelmola et al., 2019; Oeppen et al., 2020; Ferrazzi and Zapp, 2020; Price, 2020].

In general terms:

> A videoconference, web conference, or virtual meeting is a reunion, enabled by video and audio technology, between two or more people, where one or more participants are not joining in person.

A participant can have three distinct roles:

- As a receiver of information, the information flow is one-way, such as in a report presentation, a conference, or a seminar (with no question-and-answer section).
- As a participant in a discussion, the individual is not the main speaker but contributes ideas or reports. Some examples are team progress reports, problem-solving sessions, or question-answer sessions.
- As the person responsible for organizing the meeting, the participant plays the role of host, moderator, or speaker.

Figure 1.1- A videoconference, web conference, or virtual meeting is a reunion, enabled via video and audio technology, between two or more people, where one or more of the participants are not joining the meeting face-to-face. Source: Photo by Bruno Wolff on Unsplash (https://unsplash.com/photos/l5-za_iUUdA)

1.3- Advantages of videoconferences

Sometimes, it is not possible to hold a face-to-face meeting. In those cases, a virtual meeting might be the only viable alternative to get the job done. However, when there are options to have either a face-to-face or a virtual meeting, companies might opt for online sessions, citing some of the following benefits:

Savings in time or cost: In videoconferences, participants do not have to waste time traveling to a meeting place. You can have a meeting with a customer in Florida, a talk with a teammate in Chicago, and a presentation of a report to a shareholder in San Francisco. You could even attend a meeting in São Paulo and, 5 minutes later, be ready for a talk in Tokyo. In a sense, you could be traveling at the speed of light.

On the same token, a meeting could include participants from different locations. You could hold a meeting with the managers of all your foreign offices without any of them having to leave their posts.

Security is another advantage. Virtual meetings eliminate the risks of traveling. Additionally, you could attend a meeting in a war zone, the Arctic, or even outer space. On March 26, 2020, heads of state of the G20 group held a videoconference to discuss the coronavirus crisis, in a bid to develop a cohesive action plan [G20, 2020]. The cost of the security personnel needed to protect a meeting with 20 heads of state would be incredible. The security cost of safeguarding the heads-of-state meeting via videoconference is zero.

The option of **inviting external speakers** is also an advantage. Sometimes, external speakers are unavailable due to time constraints or travel restrictions. A videoconference makes it possible and cost-effective for an external speaker to participate in a meeting, even for a short part of the event.

Other advantages relate to **the technology of the videoconference**. You can record the meeting so people in different time zones or unable to attend can watch it later. The technology also allows you to bring additional resources to support your arguments, such as videos, polling tools, or product demonstrations.

In short, remote meetings allow you to maximize your reach at a lower cost while minimizing disruptions to regular business operations.

1.4- Disadvantages of videoconferences

Although there are some benefits to meeting via videoconference, the technology also has drawbacks. The disadvantages of videoconferences can be organized in three categories: technology issues, human contact issues, and individual issues.

Technology issues: Videoconferences require computer audio and video equipment and a wideband internet connection. Although those technologies have substantially reduced in price in recent years, it is still necessary for everyone in the conference to have access to the equipment.

A second technology issue is that everyone must know how to use the equipment. Once again, even though technological advances make processes simpler, people still need to know how to use the software, hardware, and communication technologies required for the videoconference.

The most shocking difference between a videoconference and a face-to-face meeting is the lack of **human contact**. People are used to communicating not only with words but also with hand movements, body position, and even smells. All those media are limited when you use a computer screen to meet. Participants in videoconferences have to practically "learn a new language" to communicate within the space a computer camera covers.

Individual issues concern how people interact with technology. Not everyone is familiar with the etiquette rules for videoconferences. It is easy to find stories about people attending virtual meetings without pants, with inappropriate backgrounds, with messy homes, or with children or pets interrupting.

Another essential individual issue is the difficulty concentrating on a screen for long periods, known as virtual fatigue. "Being online doesn't allow you to look around and see different perspectives; you only have the view in front of you. It's important to take breaks, walk around, and go out for some fresh air in between meetings." [Sutherland, 2017]

A side effect of virtual fatigue is the temptation to multitask. When you are sitting at a computer, you have more opportunities to work on other projects, read the news, or respond to e-mails (which you would not have when sitting face-to-face with another person). On the same token, bringing pets to a regular meeting is unthinkable, while, if you are home sitting in front of a computer, it might not feel odd (even if it is equally distracting).

Figure 1.2- Remote meetings allow you to maximize your reach, minimizing costs and disruptions to the regular business operation. Source: Photo by Dave Weatherall on Unsplash (https://unsplash.com/photos/uY0ko-QYSwg)

1.5- What do you need for a successful remote meeting?

There are five essential elements that you must control to have a successful remote meeting:

1.- The Location: A quiet office and a bench in a park (using the WI-FI from a café across the street) are not the same. Your materials are not at hand, which makes it harder to concentrate. Following the same logic, you won't look professional if people can see a messy bed and piles of dirty clothes behind you.

2.- The Technology: In the very worst case, you can participate in a remote meeting from a smartphone, but there is an advantage in having a desk, with all your materials on a side screen available to bring to the discussion on demand, and an image of you looking professional and in control.

3.- The Meeting's Content: If you do not want your counterpart to be distracted, you should divide the discussion into segments of 6 minutes or less. That means bringing different media to support your content. You can engage the audience with questions, votes, exercises, or videos, to name a few.

4.- The Plan: Controlling the technology, your message, and all the different media required (slides, videos, voting) is complicated. Doing it live while also trying to sell your product or convey a message requires superpowers; that is, of course, unless you prepare and follow a plan and a script for the meeting.

5.- You: You are the most critical element for a successful remote meeting. Your body should be ready; you should also feel great, know your message, and follow some basic unwritten etiquette rules for remote work.

The following chapters discuss each of these elements and provide some guidance and advice to help you have successful virtual meetings..

Chapter 2

Your Location - Setting up the Room

"Mrs. Wolowitz (off) - Howard, your Froot Loops are getting soggy!
Howard - Not now!
Dr.Massimino - Who's that?
Howard - My mom. Sorry.
Dr.Massimino - No problem, Froot Loops."

Videoconference with Nasa, "The Big Bang Theory," Season 5, Episode 15, aired February 2, 2012.

2.1- Where can you go to host a videoconference?

Imagine this scene: you start a videoconference and suddenly realize that you are not wearing pants, or someone is heard in the background telling you that your Froot Loops are getting soggy. It sounds like the material for a comedy show (and it is), but if you are not careful, it is the type of error that could make you a trending topic, and not in a positive way.

The location where you originate a videoconference is as important as what you say. You need a place where you have complete control over what goes on air. Remember that a Livestream is live; there is no stopping the tape and redoing the scene.

The ideal scenario would be to use a professional studio with staff to support your conference. The second-best alternative is to broadcast from a specially set-up conference room in your office. If you do not have either option available, you will need to find a quiet, distraction-free, nice-looking, well-lit place.

Some of the critical location elements for a successful broadcast of a Livestream meeting are:

- The room
- The background
- The lights
- The furniture

2.2- The room

If you are going to attend the meeting from home, choose a room with a door you can close, preferably at the back of the house and away from home appliances and air conditioners. Selecting the rear of the house is essential because it reduces street noise. It is crucial to be away from home appliances because they might make some distracting noises. And the door is also relevant; it helps keep noise and people out.

You need reliable Internet access. If you are using a wireless connection, check that it is stable. If you are using wires, keep them out of sight.

Television studios have a sign that says "on the air." Try putting a sign that says "in meeting" or something similar, so people know to be quiet and not enter the room. However, it is a good idea not to lock the door. If, for any reason, people need to walk in, it is better if they can open the door without knocking. That way, you do not need to interrupt the session and get up from your desk to answer.

If you cannot soundproof the room, choose a room with furniture and drapes. That helps reduce echo and dampen some outside noise.

Mute your cellphone, and do the same for your home phone (do not forget to unmute them at the end). If you need an air conditioner or heating system during the meeting, make sure it runs silently. If that is an issue, try cooling or heating the room in advance. That minimizes potential sources of external noise. Place your equipment away from air vents, as they can also be a source of distracting noise.

Ceiling fans are a problem if they are noisy, block your lights, or make them swing—constant changes in light trigger automatic camera adjustments, which can be distracting.

Among the worst places to host a videoconference is a living room or a dining room. Those areas are generally open spaces. People can walk in without warning, and they are usually tricky to soundproof.

One last piece of advice. If you are only using audio, the inside of a car is an excellent soundproof environment. You can use your cell phone. Just remember to be safe. Ensure that your vehicle is in a safe place, that your engine is off, and that you are not at risk of overheating or freezing.

Figure 2.1- You need to find a quiet place, away from distractions, nice-looking, and well-lit.. Source: Photo by Luke Peters on Unsplash
(https://unsplash.com/photos/rDxfSzXyBqU)

2.3- The background

What you show behind you is crucial. At some point, people will replay your video and analyze every detail you are willing to share. If you are in an office, you risk exposing your company's secrets or teammates' projects.

If you are home, try not to show your whole house. Look professional, clean, and uncluttered. Point the camera away from the door and towards a wall, a bookshelf, or a window.

The books, pictures, or awards that you show behind you will tell the audience something about your personality. Carefully consider what your audience will see. Someone will always ask why you have that book, or such an award, and not another.

Less is more. In other words, you may be fond of all those family pictures hanging on the wall, but your clients may find them distracting. The same goes for anything that can make you look unprofessional—clutter, clothes, piles of boxes, a bed (made or unmade), and food and beverages [Withmore, 2020].

Some videoconference systems let you replace what's behind you with a picture or video. That is called a "virtual background." Most of the time, this produces low-quality images and is not advisable. The technology requires high contrast between you and your background or an evenly lit green screen behind you. If you move and the lights are uneven, there is a chance that part of you will disappear. However, if showing what lies behind you is out of the question, this might be your only alternative.

If you decide to use a virtual background, the picture you choose is fundamental. A well-known set from a movie might be fun, but it is distracting. Remember that you want to show how good your product is, not how good you are at using the technology.

If you have a window behind you, cover the light with tape or cardboard and put some drapes or shades in front. Having an intense light source behind you makes your face impossible to see.

Figure 2.2- What you show behind you is crucial. Look professional, clean, and uncluttered. Source: Photo by Wonderlane on Unsplash (https://unsplash.com/photos/6jA6eVsRJ6Q)

2.4- The lights

People won't be able to see you if your room is too dark or too bright. If you use only overhead lights, they produce some shadows beneath your eyes. Place the light source in front of you.

You can use a desk lamp or buy a set of small LED lights on a tripod. Place the light source behind the camera, above the lens level, to the side. Ideally, you should have two sets of lights. Place one behind and to the right of your camera, and the other behind and to the left. If you put the light source precisely behind the camera, it will bounce off your face directly towards the lens, and the picture will not look right. Having the lights placed at an angle makes the reflection travel in a different direction.

The reason for placing the lights above the camera is to avoid projecting a shadow behind you. If the light comes from above you, your shadow will sit below the picture frame.

If the light source is too dim, place extra lights or a lamp on your desk. If the light is too strong, try bouncing the light source on a wall before it hits you [VSee, 2010].

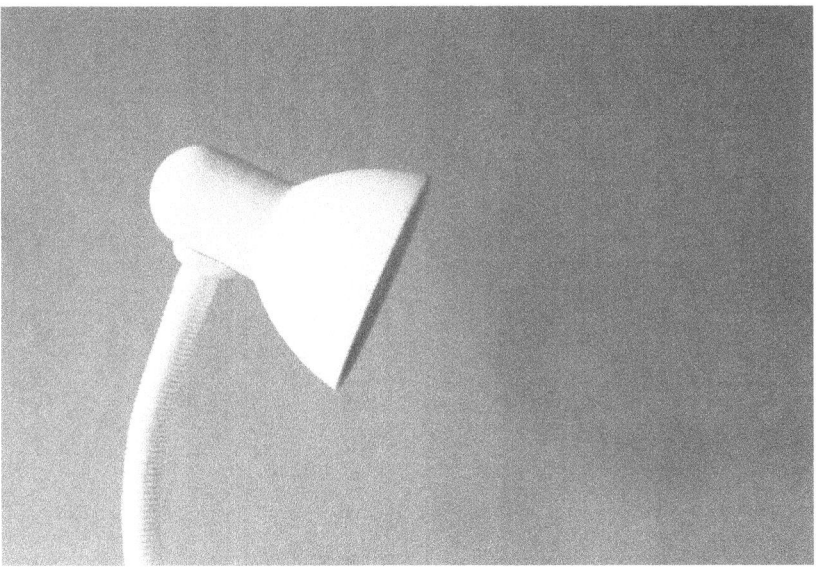

Figure 2.3- Good lighting is essential. You can use a desk lamp or buy a set of small LED lights on a tripod. Source: Photo by Manuel Sardo on Unsplash (https://unsplash.com/photos/46iThnrEw3g)

2.5- The furniture

During a videoconference, you will need easy access to all your equipment and notes. A large desk or a table makes an excellent setting for a Livestream session. The table must be steady and sturdy. It should not move, even if you accidentally kick it.

You also need a comfortable chair. Adjustable office chairs can help you position your body at the right height. However, if your body frame is too small for a large back chair, you may choose a lower back chair to avoid distraction from a chair that is too big and blocks the background.

It is a good idea to have an extra table on the side for coffee or water. This practice reduces the possibilities of spills on electric wires or electronic equipment.

Chapter 3

The Technology for a Live Videoconference

"GLENDOWER - I can call spirits from the vasty deep.

HOTSPUR - Why, so can I, or so can any man; But will they come when you do call for them?"

William Shakespeare, "Henry IV," 1599

3.1- The minimum equipment required

You could participate in a remote meeting with technology as simple as a regular phone call. Most videoconference systems allow participants to connect via regular phone calls by dialing a specific phone number and entering the conference ID for the conference they want to join. Of course, this is not the optimal solution, but you can use it as a last resort.

Moving up the technology scale, a smartphone with an Internet connection might let you view the video conference and participate by sharing your image. However, that alternative is, at the very least, uncomfortable, and cannot be used if you are trying to impress a client.

If you want any hope of a successful meeting, the minimum equipment you need is a computer with a webcam and a good Internet connection.

However, having some extra equipment can make your life easier and help your meeting go as planned.

3.2- Camera

If the computer has an integrated camera, it will sit on top of the screen. That is the best position for the camera because it allows you to maintain eye contact while still letting you see what's on your screen. A portable camera should also sit atop the monitor to maximize eye contact.

Remember that you are looking straight out of your audience's screen if you look directly into the camera lens. Talk to the camera, and you are talking to your clients. If you look at your little picture on the computer screen, you are looking away from your audience.

The camera should sit at eye level. Your table is almost certainly going to be lower than your face. You can place some books below your computer to keep your camera at the same level as your eyes. You don't want people to feel like they are looking up or down at you [Farsace, 2020].

When you frame your image on the screen, divide the screen into three horizontal segments. Your eyes should sit on the line between the top and central sections. There should be one-third of the picture above your eyes and two-thirds below.

3.3- Your computer screen (your desktop)

If you need to share your screen during a conference, take a few seconds to prepare before you hit that share button. Clear your desktop of any extra tabs or programs you may have open and make sure any private or sensitive information is hidden [Chaudhry, 2020].

3.4- Second screen

It is a good idea to organize your meeting resources (presentations, videos, spreadsheets) so you do not waste time looking them up. One way to do that is to have a second screen and declare it an extension of your current screen. On that screen, you can organize the resources; that way, you do not lose time when you need them. Drag and drop the item you need onto your main screen to share with the audience.

If you are using Windows, the command to declare the second screen as an extension of the current one is: Right-click any empty area of your desktop, then click Display Settings. This action opens the settings window. Scroll down until you see the Multiple displays pull-down menu. Click the Multiple Displays drop-down list, and then select Extend these displays. Scroll to the top of the Display Settings page. Switch the numbered boxes depending on whether your extra screen is on the right side or left side of your computer. That way, you can move your mouse to the end of your computer screen, and once you pass that point, you are on the second screen.

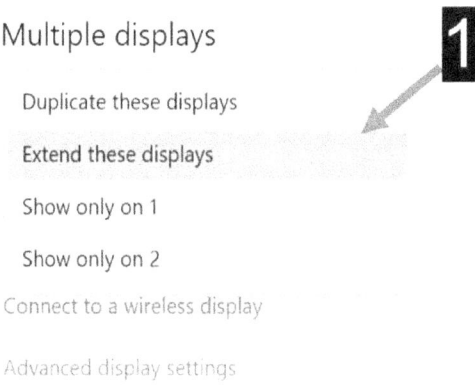

Figure 3.1- Selecting the second screen as an extension of the main screen

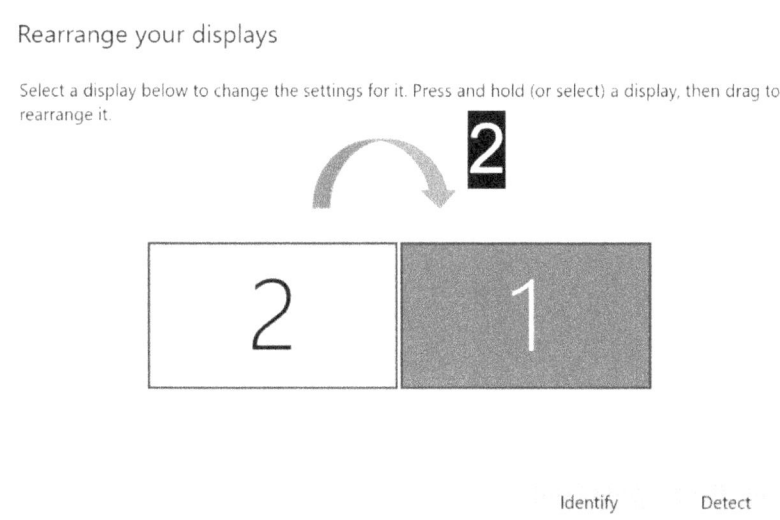

Figure 3.2- Rearranging multiple screens

During a videoconference, you can choose which screen to share. If you select the main screen, the second screen remains out of the view of the participants.

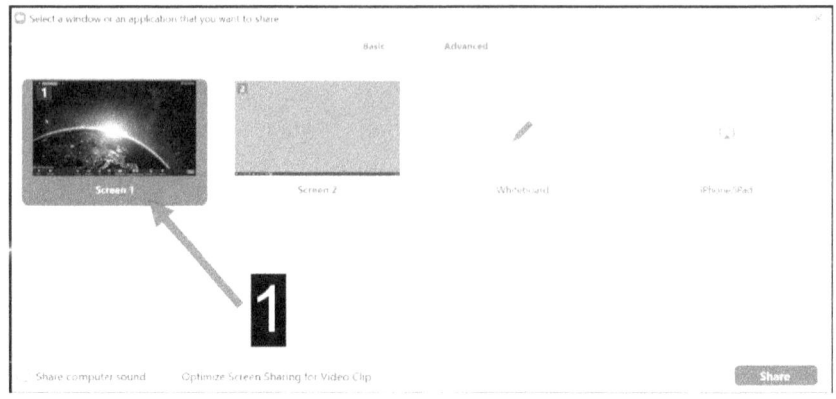

Figure 3.3- Sharing screen 1 using Zoom

3.5- Clock

It is essential to keep track of time. Your PC clock (located in the bottom-right corner of your Windows screen) is not always visible. Your cell phone may need to be tapped before it can show you the time. A better solution is to have a regular analog clock on a wall in front of you, or a small digital clock on your desk within your view. It is a crucial part of videoconference equipment. It helps you stay on track with the plan defined in the session's script.

3.6- A second PC

A second PC is not the extra screen mentioned above. This section discusses having a second computer (or a tablet) on your desk and connecting it as an attendee to your meeting. That way, you know what your clients are watching. If a video does not open or you forget to turn your camera off, your second computer will display the picture your audience sees. This way, you can fix many problems before they get out of hand.

An added value of a second PC is that it can serve as a backup in case there is a problem with your standard equipment.

3.7- The timer on a smartphone

If you have a long meeting and you need to call for a break, it is convenient to have a timer to remind you when to return to your station and restart the session. The timer function on your smartphone can tell you when to take your place after a short break. Set the timer a minute or two before the recess is over; that way, you are sure to be on time to restart the meeting.

3.8- An overhead camera for notes

If you have a smartphone (or tablet) connected to your computer via a cable, you can share the phone's screen. If you are using Zoom, use the "Share Screen" menu and select the iPhone/iPad instead of "Screen 1". The only issue is that the first time you do this, the computer might need to download some software, and the phone needs to activate the duplicate screen option. Test the technology before your meeting.

Sharing the screen of a cell phone can give you an additional camera for your materials. That function is essential when you want to show a piece of equipment, a document, or a page from a book sitting on your desk. Setting your phone on a tripod and pointing it down at the table can create a space you can share with your audience.

Just remember to disconnect the phone before moving it, or you might end up showing more of your house than you originally planned.

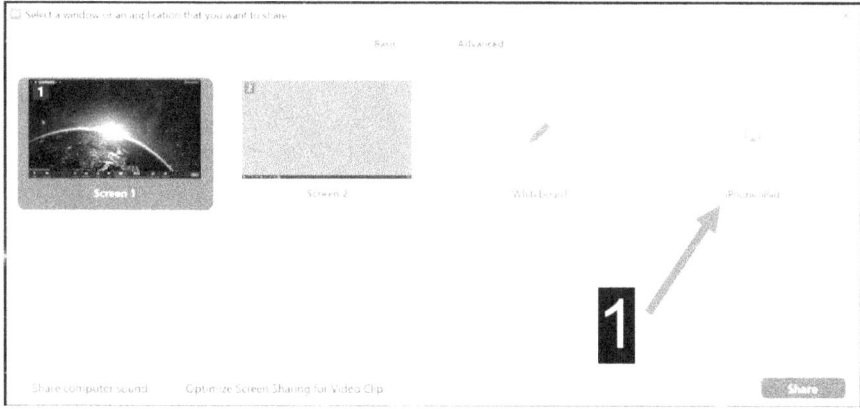

Figure 3.4- Sharing an iPhone or iPad screen using Zoom

3.9- Documents and notes

While you can keep most documents on your second screen, ready to share, one document you should print and keep on the desk during a Livestream session is the script (or session plan). That way, it is easier to know where you are in the program and how much material you still have left. It helps you control the time and pace of your presentation. Chapter five discusses how to prepare a script for an online meeting.

Chapter 4

Contents and Resources for Livestream Sessions

"To make oneself interesting artificially, that is, interesting to those who have no interest in us, is indeed a very difficult task; and to arrest the attention hour after hour, and year after year, not of one, but of a multitude of persons who have nothing in common with us, not even years, is indeed a superhuman undertaking. Yet this is the task of the teacher, or, as he would say, his "art": to make this assembly of children whom he has reduced to immobility by discipline follow him with their minds, understand what he says, and learn; an internal action, which he cannot govern, as he governs the position of their bodies, but which he must win by making himself interesting, and by maintaining this interest."

Maria Montessori, "Spontaneous Activity in Education," 1917

4.1- Improving your game

Everyone should try this: record one of your online meetings in full, sit at your desk, and watch it. You cannot have any distractions. You cannot stop the recording, make any comments, or fast-forward any part.

The first thing that comes to mind is, "My hair is wrong." Then you start questioning your smile, why you said something, or where you want to go with a particular argument. After fifteen minutes, you would be willing to accept any changes to your presentation style in exchange for a pardon from having to watch the rest of your meeting.

Of course, this is an exaggeration, but you should try it. It might help you improve your game. Professional sports players watch recordings of their previous games to find opportunities.

If you can't watch your videoconference in full, you can't expect your customers to pay attention for long.

In regular television, movies, or YouTube videos, you rarely see someone's face for more than five minutes. A ten-minute YouTube video is too long. Newscasts do not keep the camera on the anchorperson for more than a few seconds before switching to another reporter, a chart, or a video. Following the same pattern, an online meeting can start with the host commenting on something, then switch to a PowerPoint slide, a YouTube video, or a question for the participants. Some tools can be used during an online meeting to help the presenter make the session more dynamic and achieve better results. Many of those tools are also helpful for face-to-face meetings. Some require specific technology available only during a video conference, but can be adapted to work in person.

This chapter discusses the resources available for an online meeting that can help bring variety to the Livestream session and encourage the participation of your counterparts.

4.2- Before the session starts

Waiting room

Some popular videoconferencing applications, such as Zoom, have a feature called "the waiting room." The videoconference can be programmed so everyone joining can join the main videoconference, or go to a waiting room and wait for the host to let them in. Institutional users can configure the system so that participants with corporate accounts are directed to the videoconference, while those with foreign accounts start in the waiting room.

The value of this feature is that you can have control over who can enter your session. If anyone is allowed in, your meeting can fall victim to a zoombomber, a term popularized in 2020 that refers to a person entering the videoconference to cause disruption. By identifying all participants, you can screen unknown users, reduce the risk of noise or inappropriate content invading your meeting, and prevent spies from stealing your information.

A strong sense of community will enhance your online meetings. That community works better when you take measures to keep it safe from intrusion or disruption [University of Minnesota, 2020].

Late arrivals

Another design decision is whether to allow people who arrive late to a meeting. The system can be programmed to prevent anyone from connecting to the videoconference once it has started, send them to the waiting room, or let them in whenever they arrive.

The decision to block late arrivals might help maintain continuity in the discussions and foster discipline. It is a meeting design decision that must be explicitly stated in the invitation and applies primarily to internal sessions [Carnegie Mellon University, 2020]. However, keep in mind that technical issues or a lack of experience with the videoconference software might make someone unintentionally late.

4.3- Starting the session

Recording the session

If the agreement with the participants is that you will be recording the session, this is the time to start. In Zoom, the recording can be initiated or temporarily paused with a control on the top of the screen, as shown in Figure 4.1.

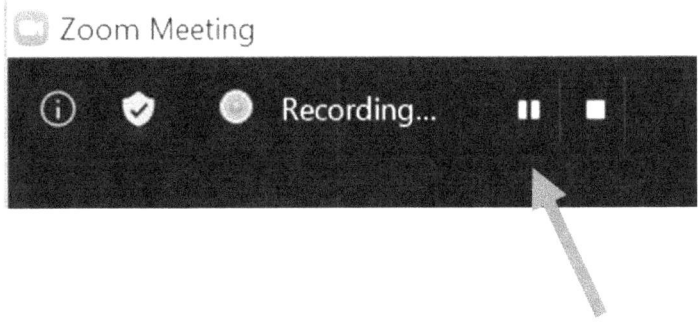

Figure 4.1- Controls for recording a session in Zoom

Intro clip

In a face-to-face meeting, when participants arrive early in the conference room, they might start informal conversations with the host or with other attendees. At some point, to signal the beginning of the meeting, some hosts close the doors, others turn on the screen projectors, or say, "ok, good morning, let's get this meeting started."

In a videoconference, a similar phenomenon can be observed. A host can activate the meeting early and start informal conversations with the participants. Once everyone is connected or at the agreed start time, a signal must indicate that the session has formally begun.

One alternative is to do the same as in a regular meeting and start by saying: "ok, good morning, let's start this meeting." This way, participants know they must shift from an informal conversation to a business meeting.

A second alternative is to start with a message to identify the lecture (especially if it is going on tape): "Welcome, I am <name>, and this is <name of the meeting>. Today is <date>." An advantage of this alternative is that you start the recording by identifying the content and the date.

A third alternative is to use a short introductory video for the meeting. Intro clips should be no longer than 15 seconds and include the meeting name and topic. Some companies have standard intro clips available. Some can show your meeting information. If you do not have an introductory clip on hand, you can produce your own using various online applications (some free). Figure 4.2. shows two screenshots of an intro video produced with Free Intro Maker. Some tools are:

- Panzoid (www.panzoid.com/tools)
- Flizpress (www.flixpress.com)
- Free Intro Maker (www.freeintromaker.com)
- Biteable (www.biteable.com/intro)
- Ivipd (www.ivipd.com)

Figure 4.2- An example of an old movie style countdown intro made with freeintromaker.com

4.4 Host's lecture

Once the meeting starts, the host can begin by introducing the participants or by allowing each participant to say a few words. The session can also start by summarizing results from previous meetings, discussing the agreed commitments, or introducing new topics. In any case, the host's participation should be in short segments of 5 to 10 minutes (and no more than 15 minutes at a time). Remember that participants in a videoconference have a limited attention span. Concentrating on a small screen is tiresome, and there is always the temptation to engage in other activities while at a meeting.

Figure 4.3- Hosts should participate in short segments, no longer than 15 minutes.

Support your presentation with PowerPoint slides or by writing on an electronic board. You can use a regular-sized whiteboard placed behind you, but make sure that the participants can see your writing. It is common to use letters that are too small or ink that is too light to show on the screen. Another alternative is to write on a piece of paper on your desk and use an overhead camera (or your cell phone) to show your diagrams (chapter three explains how to share your cell phone's screen during a videoconference).

Encourage attendants to participate, ask questions, or present support videos to make the meeting more interesting. Chapter five presents a way to organize a live session and to prepare a script to guide the discussion.

Check that your picture looks fine, your sound quality is good, and there are no distractions. Chapter two discusses how to prepare the room to increase the quality of your broadcast and minimize interruptions.

4.4.1 PowerPoint slides

For excellent presenters and for very bad presenters alike, the quality of the support materials used makes no difference. Speakers will remain just as good or just as bad as always. However, regular presenters are more convincing when they use higher-quality materials [Vogel, 1986]. Since most of the people I know fall into the middle group, having great slides becomes very important.

Some companies have graphic design experts available to help produce professional-quality presentations (see chapter seven for a discussion of this role). There are hundreds of web pages with advice on how to design better quality slides using PowerPoint if you do not have access to a graphic designer (e.g., Cartwright, 2020; Culver, 2020; Paradi, 2009; Resilient Educator, 2020; Reynolds, 2020)

Most advice for improving your slides focuses on the content, design, and delivery of your presentations. The 12 most voted recommendations are:

Figure 4.4- Slides or videos can support a presentation.

Recommendations about the content of the slides:

1. Keep your audience in mind: write slides in a language and level of detail commensurate with your participants' background.
2. Organize your presentation: Give your counterparts a message to take home, and use that idea to guide your discussion. The introduction and conclusions are critical. People remember the first and last things you tell them more vividly than the middle parts. A good opening and a proper closing will help you get your message across. Tell them what you are going to tell them, then tell them, then tell them what you told them.
3. Keep your slides simple: One message per slide, three to five bullets per slide (never more than nine points), up to five to nine words per line.
4. *Participants expect to hear from the speaker, not from the slides. Use the slides as talking points to drive your explanations. Do not read from the presentation. You do not need to include every detail in every slide. Sometimes, graphics and figures are better than words.*

Recommendations about the design of the slides:

1. Use simple designs: Stick to one color palette (light in the back and dark in the front). If the auditorium is dark, use dark background colors and light text colors.
2. Use large, simple fonts: Your font should be at least 24 pt. Large letters are easier to read, which forces you to keep the amount of information low (see recommendation 3). For slide presentations, a sans-serif font works best.
3. Use pictures, diagrams, and videos embedded in your presentation. You can stop a slideshow and call a video, but if you know when you will use the video, it is best to include it in the presentation. Make sure all graphics are of the highest quality.
4. Avoid using animations: unless necessary, do not use them in your slides. It takes too much time, distracts, and adds little value. People need to understand your ideas, not PowerPoint animation techniques.
5. Align all the objects in your slides: Learn how to use PowerPoint objects and SmartArt. You also need to know how to use the Arrange button.

Recommendations for the presentation of the slides:

1. Use the slide sorter (or print your slides six to a page): this helps you see the flow of your message across the presentation, and fix it if it does not make sense. If you print the page, you can write notes for your presentation and use it to guide you.
2. If you do not need a slide for your explanation, you can fade to black or stop sharing your screen and switch back to your PC camera for a while.
3. Practice, practice, practice.

4.4.2- Support videos

During the meeting, you can use videos to discuss specific topics or to present real-life cases from other clients. The videos must be short, lasting two to three minutes, and never more than ten. If the video is too long, it is better to show it offline and not waste the precious time available for a live session.

If you are using Zoom for your videoconference, make sure participants can hear the audio. By default, your computer's sounds are not sent to participants; only the audio from your microphone is. To let your audience view and listen to a video playing on your computer, you must share your screen. The steps are:

1. Select the screen share menu (by clicking in the bar that appears on top of your screen)
2. Select the more button (…)
3. Move your mouse down the pop-up menu, select the Share computer sound option.

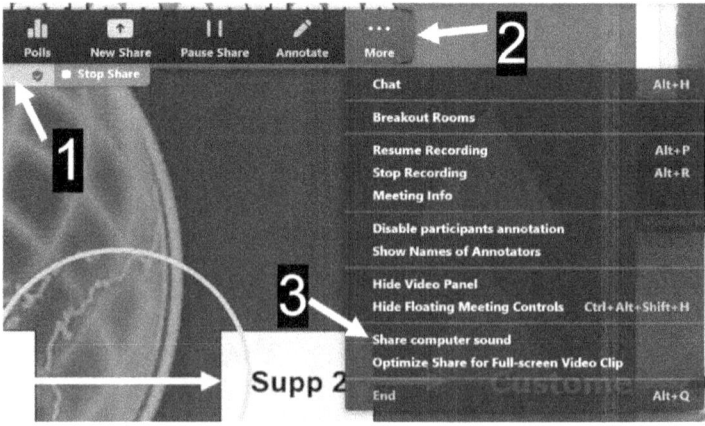

Figure 4.5- Steps for sharing your computer's sound during a videoconference while using Zoom.

4.4.3- Presentations from other team members

If the meeting plan includes presentations from other members of your team, you can assign co-hosting privileges for that portion of the meeting to the teammate presenting, while retaining control in case something goes wrong or the discussion goes off-topic. The other members might show videos, but it is generally best if the host receives the presenter's videos in advance and runs them from his/her workstation, to reduce the risk of technical problems. Some people might not have enough Internet speed at home to broadcast video in a conference.

4.4.4- Pooling the audience (voting)

Sometimes the easiest way to encourage group participation is to request a vote. In small groups with two-way video, the speaker can pose a question and ask for a raise of hands during the Livestream.

Figure 4.6- Voting by show of hands in a small group.

In larger groups, videoconferencing systems like Zoom (zoom.us) offer voting options. The host can set up several questions to present. At the appropriate time, select the Polls button (from the Zoom videoconference menu), and the selected query appears on every participant's screen. As participants vote, the host can view the results and decide whether to share them.

A different alternative (that can work equally well for videoconferences or face-to-face sessions) is to use specialized polling software like Mentimeter (mentimeter.com). The platform lets you set up different types of questions in advance (multiple-choice or single-word). Participants use their smartphones or computers to connect to the presentation by entering the session's ID number, then answer the question presented. The group can visualize their responses in real-time. A speaker can ask a question, call for a vote, initiate a discussion, and request a second vote, comparing the results.

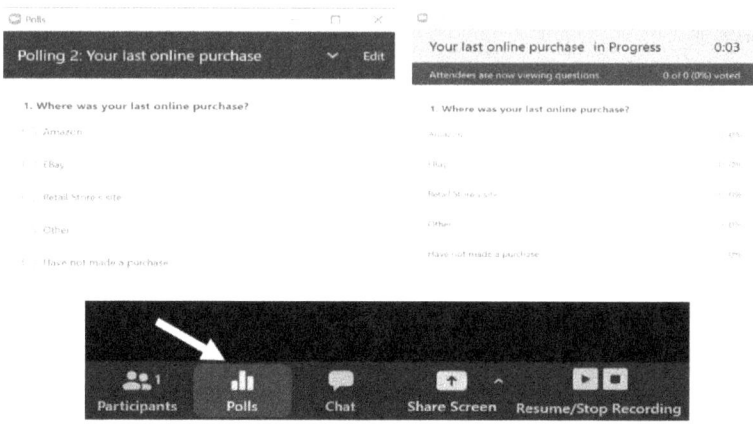

Figure 4.7- Voting during a live session using Zoom

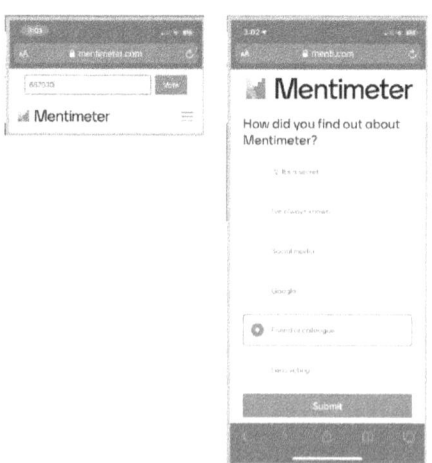

Figure 4.8- Voting on a smartphone using Menti.

Go to www.menti.com and use the code 65 79 30

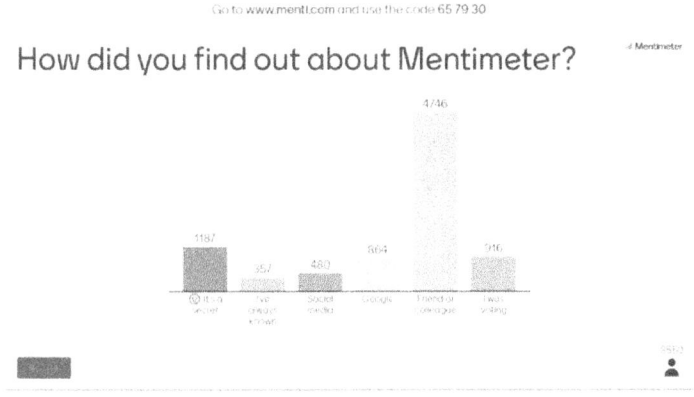

Figure 4.9- Report from a multiple-choice vote using Menti (source:
https://www.mentimeter.com/features/word-cloud)

Figure 4.10- Report from a word cloud using Menti (Source:
https://www.mentimeter.com/features/word-cloud)

4.4.5- Invited speakers

Among the advantages of remote meetings is that location is not a constraint. In
that sense, you can invite, as a guest speaker, people from anywhere in the
world. If you can arrange for a guest to participate, he/she can contribute

regardless of physical location. You have to make sure that your guest has access to a high-speed Internet connection and a computer.

Plan for a practice session to test the technology with your guest. This way, you can be sure that your guest knows what to do and that his/her equipment is ready. The practice session is also an excellent time to point out any problems with the background, camera angles, or sound.

Make sure you have a cell phone or e-mail connection in case you need to communicate with your speaker before the session or if something goes wrong during the videoconference. It is a good idea to ask your guest if you can record his/her participation to enrich your company's library of resources or use in future meetings.

4.4.6- Asking questions

During a videoconference, the speaker can post a question to the group and ask for volunteers to respond or select a participant to answer. It is better to have some informal discussion before the meeting starts, so people are familiar with the technology and lose the fear of participating in the session.

4.4.7- Answering questions

Participants sometimes have questions or need clarifications. There are several alternatives to question-answer interaction. They depend on the size of the group, the available technology, and the host's ground rules for the session.

- The host can select a time to invite the group to ask questions.
- Participants can interrupt the lecture with a question.
- Participants can signal a raised hand and wait (an option available in the meeting software).
- Participants can submit their questions to a discussion board, which the host reviews at an appropriate time.
- Participants can submit their questions to a discussion board, and an assistant can filter and forward them to the speaker.
- Participants can submit the question to a discussion board, and an assistant responds using the same media.

4.4.8- Problem solving or case discussions

It is possible to pose a problem or present a case to the group and give them time to brainstorm or find a solution. The exercise can be an individual or a group activity. To do it in groups, some videoconferencing tools, like Zoom (zoom.us), offer the option to create breakout rooms. The host decides the number of groups, assigns participants to each room, or asks the tool to make the assignments randomly. If the breakout rooms tool is unavailable, another option is to open several parallel videoconferences or discussion boards. Participants can interact in their separate discussion boards and return to the main videoconference to discuss the findings.

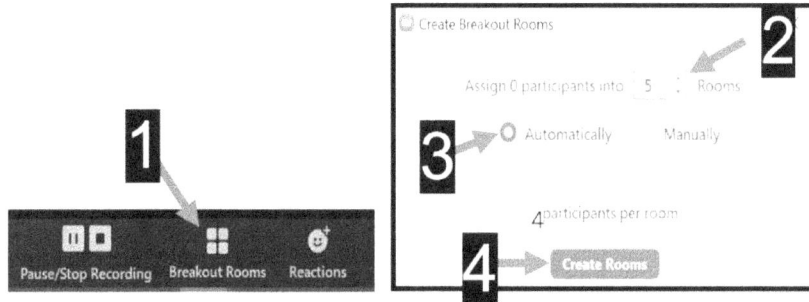

Figure 4.11- Steps for creating breakout rooms for group discussions using Zoom.

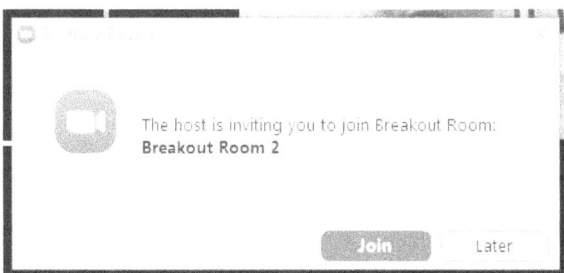

Figure 4.12- Participants must accept the invitation to join a breakout room using Zoom.

Chapter 5

Planning a Livestream Meeting

"Sesame Street was brought to you today by the letters W, S, and E; and by the numbers 2 and 3."

The closing message, Sesame Street, Episode 1, Children's Television Workshop, aired November 10, 1969.

5.1- Constraints of a Livestream session

Deciding what to include in a live remote meeting session is vital. The core of a meeting is the material that you want to share. However, there are some practical limitations to your content:

1. There is a limit to the duration of the meeting
2. Meeting time must include some housekeeping activities at the beginning and end of the session
3. There has to be some time for breaks, depending on the duration and level of your discussion
4. It would be best if you covered all the topics planned, using different types of activities
5. It is essential to divide all activities into short segments
6. Start and finish on time
7. Do not forget anything

5.2- Duration of the meeting

Regular face-to-face meetings last between 60 and 180 minutes. However, livestreaming sessions can never be that long. If you design your materials well and include appropriate breaks, you could hold a meeting for up to 2 hours, but no more. Hollywood movies, with all the technology and talent behind them, are rarely longer than 90 minutes. The movie Titanic, directed by James Cameron in 1997 and winner of 11 Academy Awards, including best picture, runs for 195 minutes [IMDb, 2020]. It is a long movie by many standards.

If it takes the best media talent in the world and a budget of 200 Million Dollars to keep you on your seat for three hours and 15 minutes, it would be a long shot to assume that a regular meeting can maintain a participant's attention for that long.

If you need more time to cover topics for your talk, consider sending some material offline or scheduling several meetings.

You also have to consider that a live session must include some space at the beginning for announcements and introductions, and at the end for closing remarks. A Livestream meeting may also need some break time in the middle.

5.3- Programming all the activities in a meeting

An online session has many events happening at the same time. The speaker is giving a lecture. At the same time, he/she must control when to share the screen, when to return, and what everyone in the meeting is doing. All the while, bringing the right resources (videos, activities, breakout rooms), answering questions, and managing the discussion board. Everything must happen in a specific sequence and without exceeding the agreed session duration.

The best way to control all the activities of a Livestream session is to have a script. A script is a document stating the sequence of events for a particular session, including timing and required technical information. Some people also call the instructions a rundown, show flow, cue2cue, q2q, or run sheet [Shoflo, 2019].

The idea is not to create a dialogue script dictating, word by word, everything that happens in the meeting. The document is a guide to help the host prepare the following resources for the session and to know precisely how much time remains.

A script is an Excel sheet with header information about the meeting, topic, and date, followed by a table with at least five columns:

- Start time
- End time
- Duration
- Description of the activity
- Resources required
- Participants

	A	B	C	D	E	F
1	Meeting id#:	AD5110 - Business Intelligence				
2	Host:	Dr. M. Alanis				
3	Topic:	Descriptive analytics and data analysis				
4						
5	Date:	05/07/2020				
6	Time:	03:00 p. m.				
7						
8	Start	End	Duration	Topic	Materials	Responsible
9	03:00	03:02	2	Start and Welcome	clip	MA
10	03:02	03:07	5	Introductions		Participants
11	03:07	03:17	10	Review OECD case	Slides S1-S4	MA
12	03:17	03:24	7	Data types	slides 1-7	MA
13	03:24	03:31	7	Data classification video	video	video
14	03:31	03:34	3	data preparation	slides 8-10	MA
15	03:34	03:40	6	Data preparation video	video	video
16	03:40	03:50	10	Statistical tests	slides 11-18	MA
17	03:50	04:00	10	Break		
18	04:00	04:12	12	Regression	slides 21-27	MA
19	04:12	04:19	7	video regression	video	video
20	04:19	04:21	2	video correlation	video	video
21	04:21	04:31	10	Data modeling	slides 28-37	MA
22	04:31	04:41	10	Case modeling	slides 38	Participants
23	04:41	04:53	12	Data visualization	slides 39-42	MA
24	04:53	04:58	5	Next meeting	LMS	MA
25	04:58	05:00	2	Closing	clip	MA

Figure 5.1- A sample script for a live stream session

The general meeting information and session identification information of rows 1 to 7 are useful because they simplify the session's start. The form gives easy access to the opening lines of the meeting: "Welcome to <meeting>, I am <name>, and today is <date>. "This is meeting #, and we will be talking about <topic>." By saying this, you create an internal timestamp for the video recording.

The next section of the script contains a table with all the activities, one per row. It includes the duration, name, resources required, and the person responsible.

The duration of the activity goes in column C. Write the time in minutes; there is no need to go down to the second. The meeting activities should be short. It is a good idea to format the column to limit the contents to a maximum value of 15. That way, if the user wants to include a lengthy activity, the Excel page would produce a warning.

Once you estimate the duration of an activity (column C), the start and end times should be calculated automatically (columns A and B). The formulas for the time column are as follows: The start time of the first activity (cell A10) is the same start time for the session (the formula can copy cell B7), or you can set the start time directly in cell A10.

The ending time equals the start time (A10) plus the number of minutes in the duration column (C10). For row 10, the finish time equals the formula =A10+time (h,m,s). The formula adds the hours, minutes, and seconds to the initial time in

A10. In this case, since C contains the number of minutes of duration of the activity, the formula for finishing time is:

$$= A10 + TIME(0, C10, 0)$$

This formula is equal to the value of A10 plus zero hours, C10 minutes, and zero seconds.

The starting time for the next row is the ending time of the previous one, so cell A11 contains =+B10. B11 copies A11, and the rest of the rows copy down the formulas to complete the table.

While revising the programming for your meeting, you might need to cut a row and paste it into a different time slot. When that happens, the formulas move. You have to be careful to maintain the time formulas unchanged. You must check the time calculations in the cells after there is a movement in the rows, or if you have to add or delete a row.

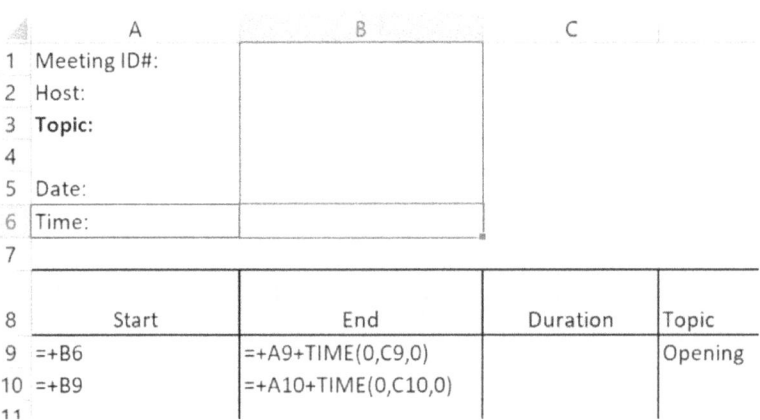

	A	B	C	
1	Meeting ID#:			
2	Host:			
3	**Topic:**			
4				
5	Date:			
6	Time:			
7				
8	Start	End	Duration	Topic
9	=+B6	=+A9+TIME(0,C9,0)		Opening
10	=+B9	=+A10+TIME(0,C10,0)		
11				

Figure 5.2- Formulas for the script page

You do not have to follow the script to the minute. It should function only as a guide, so you do not forget anything. An added advantage is that a quick look at the sheet will tell you whether you are on time, running long, or leaving some spare time at the end of the meeting.

Another recommendation about the script is to use color to identify the types of activities. Color-coding different kinds of events can help you quickly visualize the resources required for the following segment of a session.

5.4- Initial activities

All Livestream sessions start with the same activities. Five essential activities must be attended to before anything else.:

1. If you arrived early and decided to have an informal conversation before the meeting, you must tell everyone that the session is starting: "Welcome everyone, let me start the session."
2. If the agreement is that the session will be recorded, start the recording.
3. If there is an opening clip, run the clip.
4. Timestamp the session: "Welcome to <meeting> ... today is <date> ... the topic today is...". This message identifies the recording and the topics to be covered.
5. Summarize the previous meetings or agreements (two or three slides, up to five minutes).

5.5- Closing activities

Just as in the opening, the closing of a session requires some general housekeeping activities:

1. Summarize the topics covered in this session. Many people remember the famous phrase: "Sesame Street was brought to you today by the letter..." The closing summary gives the participants a way to frame what they have just learned.
2. Remind them of any agreement or pending work for the next session. Mention any special event or message that you need the group to know.
3. Respond to any housekeeping questions (e.g., weeks left before a major deadline, upcoming events, organizational changes).
4. Thank the participants for their attention.
5. If you have a closing clip, run it. If you have a credits page, show it.
6. (Wave goodbye) Close the videoconference session.
7. Stop and save the recording (Zoom automatically stops recording, converts, and saves the file when the host closes the session).

5.6- Session breaks

The duration and number of breaks required depend on the level and length of the meeting. If the session lasts 60 minutes, it could have a short five-minute break in the middle. However, 60-minute meetings that include videos and breakout activities could go without a break.

Sessions lasting 90 to 180 minutes need at least one ten-minute break in the middle. People need to refill their coffee mugs or stretch their legs.

To simplify the session restart, try to make the break coincide with an exact hour or a quarter-hour. Call a break at 9:50 to meet back at 10:00 or at 4:20 to return at 4:30.

1. Indicate that there will be a break and its length. "We will be having a 10-minute break now."
2. Indicate the time when the meeting will restart. "The meeting will reconvene at 9:30. Please do not be late."
3. Ask participants to set their phones' timers. "Please set your timers for 9 minutes so that you can be back on time."
4. If you have a slide indicating a break and the time to return, place it on the screen. If you have a video with a countdown clock, this is the time to play it.
5. Start the break. Pause the session recording, mute your microphone, and turn off your camera.
6. Shortly before the break ends, continue the recording, open your microphone and camera, and stop the countdown video.
7. Wait for people to return and continue with the session.

Do not use the break to answer questions or talk to participants. It would be best if you also relaxed a little. Take some time to double-check the materials for the rest of the session.

A word of caution. Even if you are sure that you closed your camera and muted your sound, it is a good idea to assume that they are always on. Do not make any comments, fix your hair, or change your clothes in front of a camera. If you have a wireless lapel microphone, take it out or double-check that it is off before going anywhere. The Internet is full of videos of people changing in front of a camera or having bathroom conversations in front of a live microphone.

5.7- Meeting activities

Chapter four describes the different types of activities that you can use during a Livestream session. They include the speaker's lecture, support videos, assigned presentations, problem-solving, and case discussions.

A meeting activity should be short. It should last no more than 15 minutes, but the ideal duration is 6 minutes or less. Longer activities present a challenge in maintaining participants' attention [Guo, Kim & Rubin, 2014; Berg et al., 2014].

The studies also found that:

- Interspacing images of the speaker and slides causes a better effect than slides alone.
- Drawing on a tablet or the slides has a better effect than slides alone.
- A session designed with short activities is more effective than recordings of full lectures (even if they have high quality)
- Videos in which instructors speak relatively quickly and with high enthusiasm are more effective.
- Participants view lectures and tutorial videos differently. For meetings, they focus more on the first-watch experience; for tutorials, people prefer rewatching and skimming.

[Guo, Kim & Rubin, 2014]

An additional advantage of using shorter clips is that they can be reused in similar meetings. Additionally, if they need updating, it is easier to update a six-minute clip than a two-hour lecture.

Another important aspect of your meeting activities is the variety. You cannot have all activities be the same kind or be done by the same group. When you review your script, make sure that:

- All activities last less than 15 minutes.
- There are not too many activities together of the same type, or with the same person in charge.

If your script shows all lines with the same type of activity or person responsible, your meeting might not be as effective as one with many different kinds of events.

Chapter 6

You – Etiquette for Remote Meetings

"If thou be a leader, as one directing the conduct of the multitude, endeavour always to be gracious, that thine own conduct be without defect."

The Maxims of Ptahhotep, Egypt, 2375-2350 BC. [Gunn, 1906]

6.1- General rules for any meeting

The Cambridge Dictionary defines etiquette as "the set of rules or customs that control accepted behavior in particular social groups or social situations" or as "a set of rules that helps people understand how they should behave in particular business or professional situations" [Cambridge Dictionary, 2020].

Merriam-Webster defines it as "the conduct or procedure required by good breeding or prescribed by authority to be observed in social or official life" [Merriam-Webster, 2020].

Etiquette rules go beyond common law, which generally protects people, property, institutions, and the operation of society.

Most companies have a series of rules that they apply to all their activities. They specify details such as equal opportunity, use of appropriate language, confidentiality agreements, and non-compete clauses.

For the most part, all rules for a face-to-face meeting also apply to an online one. However, there must be some minor adjustments to some rules to fit the new media. Some of the points to consider are:

1. Rules for recording Livestream sessions
2. Etiquette for e-mail communications
3. Etiquette for Livestream sessions for hosts
4. Etiquette for Livestream sessions for participants:

6.2- Rules for recording Livestream sessions

Meeting online brings the opportunity to record and share the session. Meeting recordings are useful for participants that cannot attend the Livestream for any reason. However, the risk is that meeting attendance might drop because people know that they can watch it at any other time. If participation is valuable, the host should communicate with the participants about the importance of attending the session.

The decision to save and share the session belongs to the host. If you are using Zoom, your organization can set the system to start recording from the beginning of a meeting, or when the host initiates the process. All participants see a signal when the recording starts or stops. The typical setting includes a setup to inhibit participants, other than the host, from directly recording a meeting.

It is good practice to inform participants that you plan to record the session, even if they receive a message from the system. Some organizations have recommendations to protect employees' privacy, such as allowing them to participate in audio-only (no video) or to use an alias as a screen name [Harvard, 2020].

Once the recording is complete, you can share the video by placing a link on a predefined location or sharing the link via e-mail.

6.3- Etiquette for e-mail communications

In dispersed organizations, most communication takes place via e-mail. The technology has been in use for several years, and there are countless resources offering advice on proper behavior when using it. It is a good idea to share a series of basic etiquette rules for e-mail messages with your group at the beginning of a project. The following list presents a brief overview of the rules for e-mail use in organizations. You can find more information about e-mail etiquette on any of the many sites available on the Internet. Some examples would be [Netmanners, 2020] or [University of Colorado, 2020].

Suggestions for everyone about the content of an e-mail

1. You are what you e-mail. People shape their opinion of you according to the quality of the messages you send.
2. Be formal in your writing. Check spelling and grammar,
3. Send only one topic per message; if you have two different concerns, send two notes.
4. People never scroll through messages; make sure your note fits on one screen.

5. Do not type in ALL CAPS.
6. Use words, not emojis, to send messages.
7. It is good practice to keep an e-mail account for work and a different one for personal use.

Suggestions for the host of a meeting

1. Share the meeting location, rules, and a backup phone number with the participants.
2. If you send a message to everyone, it is better to use the CCO option in the e-mail system; that way, you are not sharing your mailing list with customers or competitors.
3. If you use the CCO: option, a reply to your note won't go to everyone in the group.
4. Depending on the size of your meeting, make it a habit to respond to all messages within 24 hours (excluding weekends). People should not expect replies at 6 am for an e-mail they sent at midnight, but they should not have to wait two weeks for a response either.
5. Use formal language in your communications.

Suggestions for participants about the form of the message

1. Always use your organization's e-mail address. That way, your message is less likely to end up in the spam folder, and the organizer knows your identity.
2. The message's Subject Line must include the meeting number and topic, then one or two words about the message's matter.
3. Only send messages to the organizer about matters related to the meeting.
4. Technical questions should be addressed to the help desk (if available).

6.4- Etiquette for Livestream sessions for hosts

Consider the participant's level of expertise with the technology

Some participants may not be familiar with the technology used for hosting live videoconferences. It is a good idea to spend some time at the beginning of the meeting or during a special training session explaining how to use the system and set up the equipment.

Participants might need help learning how to open and close the camera, mute and unmute the microphones, participate in chats, and share their screen. The beginning of a project is an excellent time to go through the general etiquette rules for e-mail and live sessions. If your coworkers participate in several projects requiring remote meetings, the organization should consider offering the initial training as an orientation course for people entering the company.

Be ready for the session

Start on time - get to the session earlier to greet participants when they connect to the meeting, and let in those who start in the waiting room area of the videoconference system.

End on time - just as important as the start time is the end time of a meeting. Participants might have other commitments, and other people might be waiting to use the equipment.

Leave time for housekeeping questions – in a regular meeting, participants can approach the speaker at the end of the session to address minor issues. During a videoconference, once the meeting is over and the recording stops, you can wait a couple of minutes before disconnecting the session for a quick, informal chat with the participants.

Prepare the meeting – participants expect and deserve a well-prepared host. Prepare and follow a script. Create high-quality slides to support your points. Include some videos and a variety of activities in your meeting.

Test your equipment in advance – make sure everything works. Once everyone is connected, do not waste time with technical issues that you can resolve offline. Turn your computer on early. There is nothing more frustrating than seeing a message from Windows saying that there are 150 updates in progress and that you should wait.

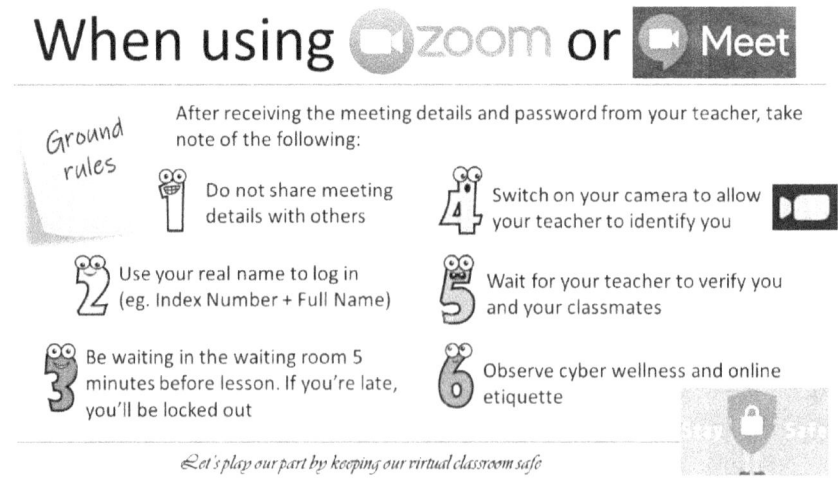

Figure 6.1- Example of a poster for students with rules for online classes from Guangyang Secondary School in Singapore [Guanngyang, 2020]

46

Dress appropriately – as you would for a face-to-face meeting. A joke about videoconferences is that you should always wear pants. There is a possibility that the camera will fall, or you will stand up in front of it.

Some specific dress codes for videoconferences: wear a shirt in a color different from your background. Preferably wear pastel colors instead of white. Remember that clothing with small vertical prints blurs on camera. If you can, use perfume or cologne. People won't be able to smell it, but they will know that you are feeling good.

Maintain eye contact by looking directly at the camera – talk to the camera, not to the participant's pictures on the screen. Participants see what your camera sees.

Assume that your camera and microphone are always on – Even if you turned them off, behave as if they were on. Never make any comments about a coworker or a competitor while they are close to the computer. If you are wearing a wireless lapel microphone, take it off before going to the bathroom.

Do not eat on camera: Drinking water or coffee is acceptable, but it is not pleasant to see a closeup of someone's lunch.

Do not undress in front of a camera - Always assume that someone is watching.

6.5- Etiquette for Livestream sessions for participants

When universities had to switch to online courses in response to the COVID-19 pandemic, many posted recommendations for messages that online class teachers could send to students. Some schools designed posters with general etiquette rules, such as [Stanford, 2020] and [Guangyang, 2020] (see figures 6.1 and 6.2). On a page with best practices for online teaching, Harvard University posted a message that the teacher could customize to inform students of the rules for online sessions. The text reads as follows:

> "Our class will meet through the Zoom online conference system. We will adopt the same rules and norms as in a physical classroom (take notes; participate by asking and answering questions; wear classroom-ready clothing). For everyone's benefit, join the course in a quiet place. Turn on your video. Mute your microphone unless you are speaking. Close browser tabs not required for participating in class. This form of learning will be somewhat new to all of us, and success will depend on the same commitment we all bring to the physical classroom." [Harvard, 2020-b]

Some of the rules applicable to participants of online meetings are:

Be ready for the online session

- o   Test your equipment in advance – make sure everything works
- o   Dress as you would for a face-to-face meeting

During the session

- o   Do
  - o   Arrive on time for the Livestream sessions
  - o   Log in using the official corporate account
  - o   Set your real name on the system (so the host can identify you)
  - o   Keep your camera on all the time (so the host can identify you)
  - o   Keep your microphone off unless you are asking a question or responding to something
  - o   Close everything not related to the meeting

- o   Don't
  - o   No eating during the meeting (coffee is ok)
  - o   No watching the session while driving
  - o   No attending the session in bed
  - o   No pets
  - o   No working on material not related to this meeting .

Figure 6.2- Poster from Stanford University with recommendations for videoconferences [Stanford, 2020]

Chapter 7

Backup Plans

"055:55:20 Swigert: ...we've had a problem here. [Pause.]

055:55:28 Lousma: This is Houston. Say again, please.

055:55:35 Lovell: [Garble.] Ah, Houston, we've had a problem. We've had a Main B Bus Undervolt."

Astronauts onboard Apollo XIII reporting an incident to Mission Control, April 1970, [Woods et al., 2017].

7.1- Analyzing risks

Most of the time, a well-planned Livestream conference works like a clock. All pieces fall into place at the right moment. The participants enjoy the experience, and you get your message across. However, if anything should fail, it is your reputation that is at stake.

You can prepare for every possible contingency; however, maintaining redundant connections and emergency plans for everything is expensive. To decide where to put your money, you can classify risks by the severity of their effects and by the probability of them happening.

Some problems are more critical than others. For example, if your Internet fails, your videoconference is over unless you have a backup connection (a cellular or satellite link) or a backup plan (go somewhere else). On the other hand, if your chair is uncomfortable, you can continue the meeting and replace it later.

Frequency is also an issue. If your electricity fails once a week, it might make sense to buy an emergency generator. On the other hand, if you live in an area where power supply is guaranteed, you can probably assume that power will not go out in the middle of your videoconference.

7.2- Managing risks

Managing risks is a three-step process:

1. Risk identification
2. Risk qualification
3. Risk reduction

When you identify something that can go wrong, the first step is to visualize the effect of that event on your videoconference and assess the likelihood of it occurring.

You can use Figure 7.1 to classify the risk. The upper-right quadrant is for issues that are likely to occur and disrupt your videoconference. In those cases, you must reduce the probability or the effect of the event. You will need to invest in a backup that can be used just in case it becomes necessary.

If, on the other hand, the event falls in the lower left quadrant (something that probably will not happen or that will have no adverse effect on the videoconference), you can ignore it. If the risk materializes, you can live with it.

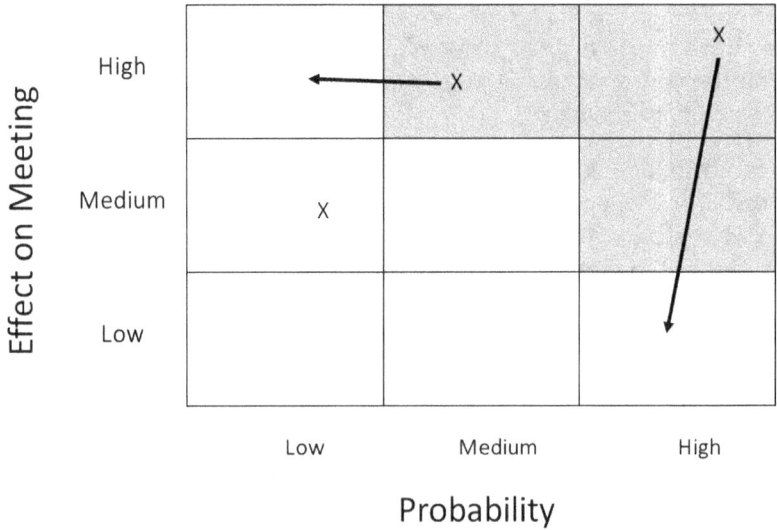

Figure 7.1- Risk classification and management matrix [Alanis, 2020]

All the events falling in the middle portion of the chart might require some planning and preparation, but not an investment in backup equipment.

Should I buy a backup computer and pay for two independent Internet connections? That depends on how often your computer or your Internet fails.

Do I need to have a backup table in case something happens to my desk? Probably not (unless your desk is about to collapse).

7.3- Some precautions if you are attending a videoconference

If you are a participant in a videoconference, most location problems are easy to fix:

- If your lights do not work, you can bring a desk lamp or a table lamp to the room.
- Desk or chair failures are relatively easy to fix. Most people have extra chairs or tables in the house.
- If you definitely cannot show what is behind you, try working in front of an empty wall, or use a virtual background.

Some more complicated problems during a Livestream:

- If there is suddenly a noise that you cannot stop: if you are not talking, mute your microphone; and when it is time to talk, get close to the microphone.
- If you are not presentable, do not use video.
- If you realize you are not wearing pants or have another wardrobe problem, stop the video first, then go find some clothes.
- If someone suddenly walks into the room, close the camera (or physically put a Post-it note or a piece of paper over the camera lens)
- If you have a poor Internet connection, try connecting with audio-only.

If the Internet fails, plan with a neighbor to share his/her Internet connection, or locate a nearby Internet café or public Internet link.

7.4- Additional measures if you are a presenter

Things can go wrong during a presentation. You can lose your slides, or programs can stop running.

- If a YouTube video is not running, you can skip it, explain its contents, and send a link later so people can watch it.
- If your Internet connection is too slow, disconnect video from everyone; if necessary, you might even disconnect your video.
- If you are starting late or have to stop the meeting, post a sign on your screen explaining the problem and share your screen (don't forget to mute your microphone).

If you need to cancel or cannot start the videoconference, you need to communicate with everyone:

Set up a trusted communication channel (e.g., an e-mail) where participants can check for any issues.

In extreme cases, consider using your telephone instead of a videoconference. Some phone lines (or some services) offer the option of connecting multiple callers simultaneously into a phone call.

7.5- Test everything before it is too late

The most valuable risk mitigation advice is:

- Test everything in advance

Run a trial for the video conference. Practice with the guest speakers before the meeting to ensure their computers and connections are up to par. Connect to the videoconference early so you have time to fix any issues before the session starts.

Finally, do not forget to stay calm, smile, and have a good time.

Chapter 8

The Value of Support Staff

"Thank you so much. This is an amazing honor. Thank you, Academy. To create a single frame of film, as you well know, requires the work of a lot of people, a very hard work. So, I want to thank Yalitza Aparicio and Marina de Tavira, before anybody else; the amazing cast and crew; Gabriela Rodríguez and Nicolás Celis as producers; Participant and Netflix; Technicolor and Arri"

Alfonso Cuaron, Acceptance Speech, Best Cinematography, for the movie "Roma," 91st Academy Awards, February 24, 2019.

8.1- I would like to thank my producer, my graphic designer, and my assistants…

A Hollywood film costs millions of dollars to produce and requires a wide range of experts, including directors, actors, sound editors, makeup artists, and more. If you watch the very end of a film, you can see a list of hundreds of people who worked on the project.

A remote meeting, or even a conference, never has that kind of budget. Most of the time, the speaker is responsible for designing the session, preparing the slides, managing the technology, delivering the speech, and answering questions.

The speaker is an expert in his/her field. No one can do a better job of selling a service or negotiating a contract with a potential customer. But being good for business does not generally prepare you to manage audiovisual equipment, configure communications software, or design great slides.

One of the reasons some people fear working online is that it is hard enough to sell something, let alone learn and worry about so many other technical matters. Of course, technology has advanced significantly, and anyone can hold a video conference. But it could be easier if the host had some help along the way.

Some companies have a technology expert on staff to help resolve configuration and communication issues. Other organizations go so far as to have a videoconference factory, a division responsible for producing and supporting every aspect of a distance meeting. Most offices are somewhere in the middle.

Among the roles most relevant for the design and management of remote meetings are: [Alanis, 2003; Ferran et al., 2019]

- Speaker/host
- Help desk
- Graphic designer
- Producer
- Assistant

8.2- The speaker / host

The host has two roles in remote meetings: designing and delivering the meeting content. A well-designed videoconference can make it more enjoyable for the speaker and the attendees.

The host can enlist the help of different people for the overall design of the videoconference activities, the production of support videos, and the preparation of support materials.

The host is ultimately responsible for the event's design. He/she must ensure everyone on the staff knows the deadlines and deliverables, share the production calendar, and hold startup and periodic progress meetings [Stanford Center for Professional Development, 2020].

8.3- Help desk

One of the most time-consuming activities in a remote meeting, unrelated to the meeting's subject, is troubleshooting technical issues. Attendees have all sorts of technical problems during a video conference. They range from forgotten passwords to computer viruses to slow Internet connections. It is essential, especially if the organization commits to remote work, to have a well-trained, readily available help desk to resolve technical issues for meeting participants.

Help desks can also offer courses on using the videoconference software or other technical matters. If people know where to get help with technical issues, the host can spend more time on relevant work for the meeting.

8.4- Graphic designer

It is crucial to have quality support materials. They help add credibility to a presenter [Vogel, 1986]. A graphic designer is a specialist who can help define requirements, visualize, and create your slides [Workable Technology Limited, 2020]. The graphic designer is responsible for recommending the best layout, font type, font size, and color selection to maximize the presentation's impact across various platforms.

The graphic designer does not develop the content of the presentation or web page. They work with the speaker to polish the visual aspect of the support materials.

Figure 8.1- The graphic designer works with the speaker to polish the visual aspect of the support material. Photo by Theme Photos on Unsplash
(https://unsplash.com/photos/CGpifH3FjOA)

8.5- Producer

In contrast with Hollywood film producers, a producer for a remote meeting is not responsible for financing, selecting the script, or coordinating direction and editing. In a videoconference, the speaker is responsible for the content, while the producer focuses on the product's technical quality.

A producer can assist with content development and also during the Livestream session. The producer makes all the arrangements for recording, editing, and production of the videos. You can prerecord the content in a studio with a producer, or use a personal camera and have a producer correct the image, check the sound, and edit the slides into a video. A well-produced video demonstrates quality work and attention to detail.

During a Livestream session, a producer controls the cameras, decides which shot to air, keeps track of the time, and runs the appropriate activity or video according to the script.

Figure 8.2- The producer responds to the product's technical quality. Photo by Drew Patrick Miller on Unsplash (https://unsplash.com/photos/_o6AAx9dl_Y)

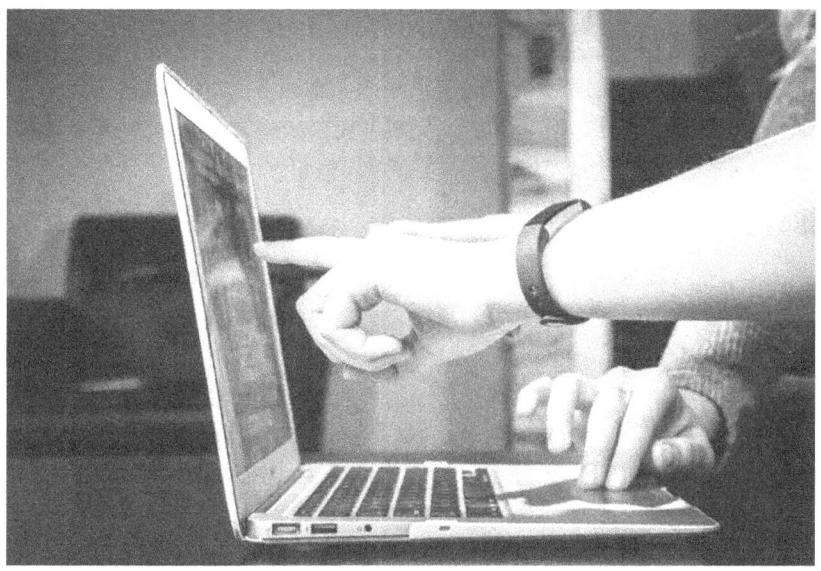

Figure 8.3- During the meeting, an assistant can help run discussion boards and answer participants' technical and operational questions.. Photo by John Schnobrich on Unsplash (https://unsplash.com/photos/FIPc9_VocJ4).

8.6- Assistants

An assistant can help during content development by collecting information, reviewing candidate videos to include, or researching specific topics.

During the meeting, an assistant can help run discussion boards and answer participants' technical and operational questions. The typical problems that an assistant can manage are:

- Can I get a copy of the slides?
- Where can I find that document?
- Where is the recording of the last session?
- I submitted the wrong file; can I change it?
- Where is the link for the live session?
- Where do I go to reset my password?

When an assistant answers these types of questions, the host has more time to focus on making substantive comments on the discussion boards or answering questions central to the meeting topic.

During a live session, an assistant can help manage the discussion board and handle technical matters if there is no producer in the room. In large groups, where the questions come via e-mail or a discussion board, the assistant filters and organizes the items sent to the speaker during the session, and might answer many of the more operational questions directly.

If the transmission runs from a production cabin, the assistant knows enough about the meeting and the host to know when to switch slides without the speaker having to ask for the next one repeatedly.

8.7- Are all the roles necessary for a videoconference?

Not all the roles are necessary to produce and run a remote meeting. The only critical element is the host. In some companies, a single host must fulfill all roles. However, having access to a team of qualified professionals can help create a high-quality product that is more useful to the organization and the participants.

References

Chapter 1

[Dickens, 1859] Dickens, C., "A Tale of Two Cities," a facsimile of the original first publication of "A Tale of Two Cities" in All the Year Round, April 1859, consulted July 2020 in https://dickens.stanford.edu/dickens/archive/tale/pdf/tale_01.pdf

[Cambridge dictionary, 2020] Cambridge Dictionary, "videoconferences" consulted August 2020 in https://dictionary.cambridge.org/dictionary/english/videoconferencing

[Fadlelmola, et al., 2019] Faisal M. Fadlelmola, F. M., Panji, S., Ahmed A. E., et al. "Ten simple rules for organizing a webinar series" PLOS Computational Biology, 15(5), April 2019, consulted September 2020 in https://doi.org/10.1371/journal.pcbi.1006671

[Ferrazzi and Zapp, 2020] Ferrazzi, K., Zapp, S., "The Upside of Virtual Board Meetings," Harvard Business Review, July 2020, consulted September 2020 in https://hbr.org/2020/07/the-upside-of-virtual-board-meetings

[G20, 2020] G20 Saudi Arabia 2020, "G20 Extraordinary Virtual Leaders' Summit on COVID-19 to be held on Thursday" consulted August 2020 in https://g20.org/en/media/Documents/G20_Statement_King%20Salman%20Virtual%20Summit_EN%20(1).pdf

[Merriam-Webster, 2020] Merriam-Webster, "Videoconference" consulted August 2020 in https://www.merriam-webster.com/dictionary/videoconferencing

[Oeppen et al., 2020] Oeppen, R. S., Shaw, G., Brennan, P. A., "Human factors recognition at virtual meetings and video conferencing: how to get the best performance from yourself and others" British Journal of Oral and Maxillofacial Surgery, Volume 58, Issue 6, pp 643-646, July 2020, consulted September 2020 in https://doi.org/10.1016/j.bjoms.2020.04.046

[Price, 2020] Price, M., "Scientists discover upsides of virtual meetings," Science, May 2020, 368(6490), pp 457-458, consulted September 2020 in https://science.sciencemag.org/content/368/6490/457.full

[Rubinger et al, 2020] Rubinger, L., Gazendam, A., Ekhtiari, S. et al. "Maximizing virtual meetings and conferences: a review of best practices." International Orthopaedics (SICOT), Vol. 44, PP. 1461–1466 (2020). Consulted September 2020 in https://doi.org/10.1007/s00264-020-04615-9

[Sutherland, 2017] Sutherland, L., "157 – The Disadvantages Of Video Conferencing" Collaboration Superpowers, August 2017, consulted September 2020 in https://www.collaborationsuperpowers.com/157-the-disadvantages-of-video-conferencing/

[Wikipedia, 2020] Wikipedia "web conferencing" consulted August 2020 in https://en.wikipedia.org/wiki/Web_conferencing

Chapter 2

[Lorre et al., 2012] Lorre, C., Kaplan, E., & Reynolds, J. (Producers) Cendrowski, M. (Director), "The Big Bang Theory" Season 5, Episode 15, "The Friendship Contraction" CBS, Aired February 2, 2012, consulted June 2020 in https://bigbangtrans.wordpress.com/series-5-episode-15-the-friendship-contraction/

[VSee, 2010] VSee, "Don't Forget Lighting! part 1" VSee, 2010 consulted June 2020 in https://vsee.com/blog/video-conference-lighting-tips-part-1/

[Withmore, 2020] Withmore, J., "7 Essentials for Looking Your Best in Video Conference Calls", Entrepreneur, consulted June 2020 in https://www.entrepreneur.com/article/294107

Chapter 3

[Chaudhry, 2020] Chaudhry, A., "The Do's and Don'ts of Video Conferencing" The Verge, March 19, 2020, consulted June 2020 in https://www.theverge.com/2020/3/19/21185472/video-confere-call-tips-zoom-skype-hangouts-facetime-remote-work

[Farsace, 2020] Farsace, B, "How to Look Your Best on a Video Call" The Verge, April 8, 2020, consulted June 2020 in https://www.theverge.com/2020/4/8/21202907/zoom-tips-video-call-lighting-audio-look-your-best

[Shakespeare, 1599] Shakespeare, W., "Henry IV, part 1" 1599, Consulted June 2020 in http://shakespeare.mit.edu/1henryiv/full.html

Chapter 4

[Carnegie Mellon University, 2020] Eberly Center - Teaching Excellence & Educational Innovation, Carnegie Mellon University, "Students Come to Class Late" Carnegie Mellon University, 20202, consulted June 2020 in https://www.cmu.edu/teaching/solveproblem/strat-latetoclass/index.html

[Cartwright, 2020] Cartwright, J., "14 PowerPoint Presentation Tips to Make More Creative Slideshows [+ Templates]", Hubspot, 2020, consulted June 2020 in https://blog.hubspot.com/marketing/easy-powerpoint-design-tricks-ht

[Culver, 2020] Culver, H., "10 Easy Ways to Make any PowerPoint Presentation Awesome", hughculver.com, 2020, consulted June 2020 in http://hughculver.com/10-easy-ways-make-powerpoint-presentation-awesome/

[Montessori, 1917] Montessori, M., "Spontaneous Activity in Education" Translated from the Italian by F. Simmonds, Frederick A. Stokes Company, New York, NY, 1917.

[Paradi, 2009] Paradi, D., "Top 5 PowerPoint Tips for Student Presentations in School", Think Outside the Slide, 2009 consulted June 2020 in https://www.thinkoutsidetheslide.com/top-5-powerpoint-tips-for-student-presentations-in-school/

[Resilient Educator, 2020] Resilient Educator Editorial Team, "Teachers: 5 Tips for Creating Great PowerPoint Presentations", Resilient Educator, 2020, consulted June 2020 in https://resilienteducator.com/classroom-resources/teachers-5-tips-for-creating-great-power-point-presentations/

[Reynolds, 2020] Raynolds, G., "Top Ten Slide Tips" garryreynolds.com, 2020, consulted June 2020 in http://www.garrreynolds.com/preso-tips/design/

[University of Minnesota, 2020] The University of Minnesota, "Zoom: Teach Online Class Sessions" University of Minnesota, 2020, consulted June 2020 in https://it.umn.edu/services-technologies/how-tos/zoom-teach-online-class-sessions#community

[Vogel, 1986] Vogel, D. R., "Persuasion and the Role of Visual Presentation Support: The UM/3M Study", University of Minnesota. Management Information Systems Research Center, Working papers series, Vol. 86, No. 11, 1986.

Chapter 5

[Berg et al., 2014] Berg, R., Brand, A., Grant, J., Kirk, J., & Zimmerman, T. "Leveraging recorded mini-lectures to increase student learning" Online Classroom, 14(2), 2014, consulted June 2020 in https://www.academia.edu/6778520/Leveraging_Recorded_Mini-Lectures_to_Increase_Student_Learning

[Children's Television Workshop, 1969] Children's Television Workshop, "Sesame Street" episode 1, Children's Television Workshop, aired November 10, 1969, consulted June 2020 in https://www.youtube.com/watch?v=D7szvFGXKGg

[Guo, Kim & Rubin, 2014] Guo, P. J., Kim, J. & Rubin, R., "How Video Production Affects Student Engagement: An Empirical Study of MOOC Videos" Learning at Scale 2014, Proceedings of the First ACM Conference on Learning at Scale Conference, Atlanta GA, March 2014, consulted June 2020 in http://up.csail.mit.edu/other-pubs/las2014-pguo-engagement.pdf

[IMDb, 2020] IMDb, Inc., "Titanic (1997)", IMDb, Inc., 2020, consulted June 2020 in https://www.imdb.com/title/tt0120338/

[Shoflo, 2019] Shoflo LLC, "What Is A Production Cue Sheet?", Shoflo LLC; 2020 consulted June 2020 in https://shoflo.tv/what-is-a-production-cue-sheet/

Chapter 6

[Cambridge Dictionary, 2020] Cambridge Dictionary, "Etiquette" consulted June 2020 in https://dictionary.cambridge.org/dictionary/english/etiquette

[Guangyang, 2020] Guangyang Secondary School," Full Home Based Learning (HBL) Important Information and links for Students" Guangyang Secondary School, consulted June 2020 in https://guangyangsec.moe.edu.sg/students/full-home-based-learning-gy-online/full-home-based-learning-hbl-important-information-and-links-for-students

[Gunn, 1906] Gunn, B.G., "The Instruction of Ptah-Hotep" in "The Instruction of Ptah-Hotep and the Instruction of Ke' Gemini: The Oldest Books in the World" John Murray, Albemarle Street, Editor, London, England, 1906 consulted June 2020 in https://www.gutenberg.org/files/30508/30508-h/30508-h.htm

[Harvard, 2020] Harvard University, "Rules and Best Practices for the Recording of Classroom Sessions Conducted via Zoom" KB0016520, Harvard University, March 2020, consulted June 2020 in https://harvard.service-now.com/ithelp?id=kb_article&sys_id=6880408bdbab8c9430ed1dca489619bc

[Harvard, 2020b] Harvard University, "Best Practices: Online Pedagogy" Harvard University, 20202, consulted June 2020 in https://teachremotely.harvard.edu/best-practices

[Merriam-Webster, 2020] Merriam-Webster, "Etiquette" consulted May 2020 in https://www.merriam-webster.com/dictionary/etiquette

[Netmanners, 2020] Net M@nners, "101 E-mail Etiquette Tips", Net M@nners, consulted June 2020 in https://www.netmanners.com/email-etiquette-tips/

[Stanford, 2020] Cardinal at Work, Stanford University, "Manage the Virtual Workplace" Stanford University, consulted June 2020 in https://cardinalatwork.stanford.edu/manager-toolkit/engage/retention-strategies/managing-virtual-workplace

[University of Colorado, 2020] University of Colorado, Boulder, "E-mail Etiquette: How to Write e-mails to Your Professors" University of Colorado, consulted June 2020 in https://www.colorado.edu/amath/sites/default/files/attached-files/email_etiquette_1.pdf

Chapter 7

[Alanis, 2020] Alanis, M., "Tecnologia de Informacion y la Practica Contable", ISBN: 979861244439, 2020

[Woods et al., 2019] Woods, W. D., Kemppanen, J., Turhanov, A., Waugh, L. "Day 3, part 2: 'Houston, we've had a problem'" Apollo Flight Journal, May 2017, consulted September 2020 in https://history.nasa.gov/afj/ap13fj/08day3-problem.html

Chapter 8

[Alanis, 2003] Alanis, M., "Teaching an MIS Course Completely online" Proceedings of the 2003 International Conference on Informatics, Education, and Research," Seattle, Washington, December 2003

[Cuaron, 2019], Cuaron, A., "Acceptance Speech" Best Cinematography for "Roma" 91st Academy Awards, February 24, 2019, consulted June 2020 in aaspeechesdb.oscars.org

[Ferran, et al., 2019] Ferran C., Alanis M., Esteves J., Gomez J., Guzman I., "Online Education (AMCIS 2017 Panel Report)" Communications of the Association for Information Systems, 1529-3181, December 2019.

[Stanford Center for Professional Development, 2020], Stanford Center for Professional Development, Stanford University, "Stanford Online Course Creation Essentials: A Guide for Faculty and Instructors Transitioning to Online Instruction" Stanford University, consulted June 2020 in https://vptl.stanford.edu/teaching-online-at-stanford

[Vogel, 1986] Vogel, D. R., "Persuasion and the Role of Visual Presentation Support: The UM/3M Study", University of Minnesota. Management Information Systems Research Center, Working papers series, Vol. 86, No. 11, 1986.

[Workable Technology Limited, 2020] Workable Technology Limited, "Graphic Designer job description" Workable.com, 2020, consulted June 2020 in https://resources.workable.com/graphic-designer-job-description

About the Author

Dr. Macedonio Alanis

alanis@tec.mx   maalanis@hotmail.com

Dr. Macedonio Alanis is a Full Professor of Management Information Systems at Tecnologico de Monterrey. For over 25 years, he has been teaching face-to-face and distance learning graduate and undergraduate level courses in technology management, e-commerce, IT strategy, and e-government. Some of his distance education courses are attended live by nearly 1000 students in nine countries. He also designed and taught a dual degree program on IT Management between ITESM and Carnegie Mellon University and worked on a project management specialization program between ITESM and Stanford University.

In the private sector, Dr. Alanis has served as the manager of administration and finance at Neoris, an IT company of the multinational CEMEX (NYSE:CX). He has worked for IBM and is part of the Cutter Consortium's group of expert consultants.

In the public sector, he worked as Director of Information Technology (CIO) for the Government of the State of Nuevo Leon. He participated in the definition of Mexico's national IT policies.

Dr. Alanis has authored more than 120 papers, books, and conference proceedings. He received the prestigious Eisenhower Fellowship and was elected to occupy the Americas Chair on the Association for Information Systems (AIS).

Dr. Alanis holds a Ph.D. in Business Administration with a concentration in Management Information Systems from the University of Minnesota. He obtained a Master of Science in Computer Science (ScM) from Brown University and a BSc in Computer Science from Tecnologico de Monterrey.

www.ingramcontent.com/pod-product-compliance
Lightning Source LLC
Chambersburg PA
CBHW070508220526
45467CB00002B/603